IMAGES OF IRELAND

NORTH DUBLIN
FROM THE LIFFEY
TO BALBRIGGAN

Dubli
City F

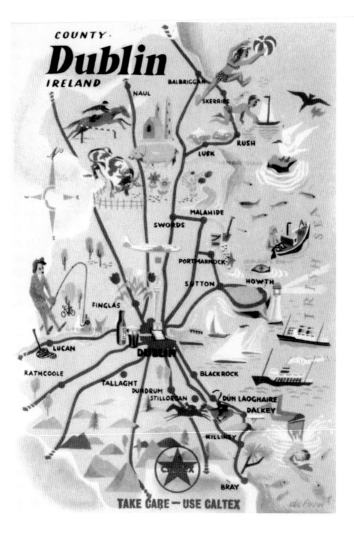

IMAGES OF IRELAND

NORTH DUBLIN
FROM THE LIFFEY
TO BALBRIGGAN

DR. DEREK STANLEY

NONSUCH

Frontispiece: Picture-map showing county Dublin, *c.*1950. The area covered in this book is shown to the north of the River Liffey. This includes the northern city suburbs and north county Dublin. The area has many historic churches and castles, picturesque villages, fine seaside resorts and Dublin Airport. Petrol companies were often associated with road maps and the postcard has the 'star in hexagon' advertising logo for the Caltex oil company.

First published 2006

Nonsuch Publishing Limited
73 Lower Leeson Street
Dublin 2
Ireland
www.nonsuch-publishing.com

© Dr. Derek Stanley, 2006

British Library Cataloguing in Publication Data.
A catalogue record for this book is available from the British Library.

ISBN 1 84588 555 4

Typesetting and origination by Tempus Publishing Limited.
Printed in Great Britain.

Contents

The River Liffey rises in the Wicklow mountains at Kippure, thirteen miles from Dublin. However, it flows in a great loop through Wicklow and Kildare, giving it a total length of seventy miles before it reaches the sea at Dublin Bay. The river bisects Dublin from west to east into the north and south sections of the city. In this view, on the right, is the Custom House, with its conspicuous dome, which is the first building, seen on the north side of the Liffey, before Butt Bridge.

Introduction

North Dublin is an area of special character which has roots in over a thousand years of history. The coastal suburbs have great natural beauty and include the cliffs of Howth, fine harbours and seaside resorts with sandy beaches and superb golf courses. Following the dissolution of Dublin County Council, Fingal County Council was established on 1 January 1994. The area of Fingal stretches from the River Liffey up along the borders of Co. Meath up to and including Balbriggan. This book includes photographs from the North Dublin City and the Fingal area. 'Fingal' is derived from the Gaelic 'Fine Gall' meaning 'foreign tribe', which recalls the Scandinavian settlement in the Fingal area during the ninth and tenth centuries.

As with my previous books on Central Dublin and South Dublin, the photographs and postcards have been chosen to give a 'flavour' of North Dublin and some of its history. It is an area of contrasts. Much has changed with time and many of the views show streets and buildings which are now completely altered. In fact, some buildings have been demolished and photographs are now the only record. It is difficult to do the area justice in a book of this size. However, there is a brief glimpse of the northern part of the city and the environs. With each image there is some narrative, which is necessarily short, but I do hope that the information adds interest. North Dublin is a unique area, but the preservation of its fine buildings has not always been a priority. Today there is much more commitment to preserving our heritage.

The area's natural beauty speaks for itself but hopefully the images in the book will bring enjoyment and help recall some nostalgic memories of people, events and places in North Dublin, which are already part of history.

Acknowledgements

I am very grateful to my friends and family, who have helped me by providing photographs, inspiration and information for this book. My thanks to Seamus Kearns for allowing me to use some postcards from his own collection. I am pleased to acknowledge and thank Joan O'Byrne, Fergal MacAllister, Kitty Brooks, Pauline Dempsey, May Kane, Kitty Quinn, Cathy O'Donaghue, Phyllis O'Dowd, Terry O'Toole, John McGarry, the late Dr. George Corbett, Dr. Aidan Hampson, Peter and Marjorie O'Hara and Des Sweeney. I would also like to thank my wife Theresa who has provided me with so much support and encouragement.

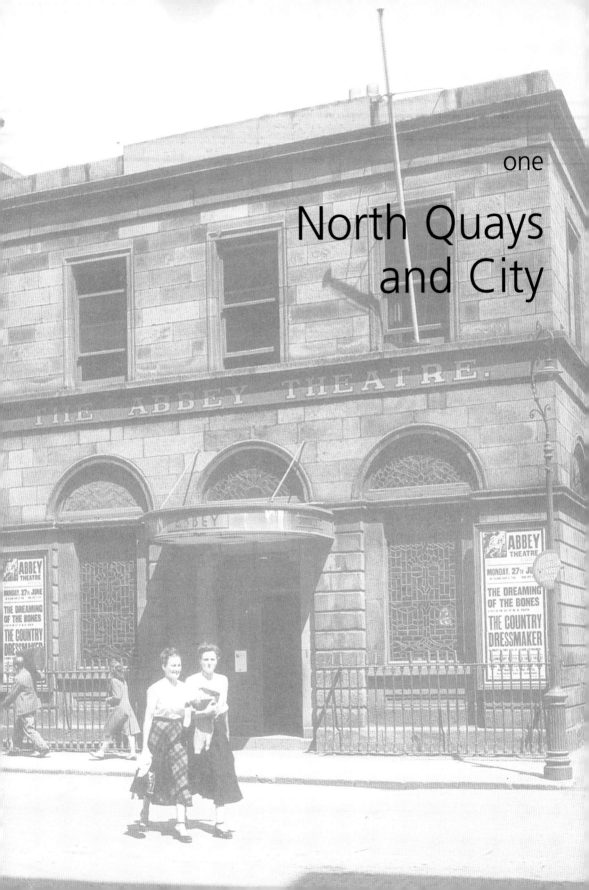

one

North Quays
and City

An aerial view of the docks at Dublin c.1950. An impressive gateway to Ireland and very large passenger and merchant ships are able to moor at the North Wall. At that time, the area available for shipping was around 230 acres and extended from Eastern Breakwater to Butt Bridge. On the north side of the river were the Custom House Docks, St George's Dock and the North Wall Quay. Over the river were the southside quays and the Grand Canal Docks near Ringsend. The main imports were coal, grain, timber and general merchandise. The main exports included cattle and Guinness. Ship repairs were carried out at the Graving Docks at the North Wall.

Paddle Steamer at Custom House Quay, Dublin, c.1900. Barrels of stout are piled on the quayside waiting to be loaded on boats for export to England. The magnificent Custom House, designed by James Gandon, was completed in 1791, having taken ten years to build and costing around £400,000. The main south front, which is made of white Portland stone, faces the river. The other three sides of the building are made of mountain granite. The building was restored after it was gutted by fire during the civil war in May 1921.

The hospital ship, *Oxfordshire*, at the North Wall, Dublin in 1914 carrying wounded soldiers returning from the Great War. A Southern Irish horse box waits to receive the patient on the stretcher. During the First World War, the hospital ships *Oxfordshire* and *Valdivia* brought a steady stream of wounded soldiers home to Dublin. Most soldiers were taken to the Dublin hospitals for treatment. However, some soldiers were brought to Dublin Castle, where the large rooms had been converted to a hospital for wounded soldiers.

Dublin Docks, *c.*1915. A wounded soldier on a stretcher is carried to a car. The members of the Royal Irish Automobile Club regularly volunteered to take wounded soldiers to hospital. Other soldiers were taken by ambulance or train. There were two trains used to carry wounded soldiers. Train number thirteen belonged to the Great Western Railway and was converted for this purpose at Dundalk. The other train came from the Great Southern and Western Railway Company and this was converted at the Inchicore works in Dublin. This company also built an ambulance car, which was forty-four feet long and carried iron bedsteads bolted to the floor. During the 1914–18 War, over 12,000 patients, who arrived by hospital ships at the docks, were carried by the two Irish trains and taken to hospitals in the Dublin area.

ROYAL MAIL SERVICE

CITY OF DUBLIN STEAM PACKET C.º
15. Eden Quay.   DUBLIN

Two services each way daily between KINGSTOWN & HOLYHEAD
in connection with the Mail Trains from all parts of ENGLAND and
IRELAND. Best and Fastest Route.

Advertising card for Royal Mail Service, City of Dublin Steam Packet Company, 15 Eden Quay, Dublin, posted on 6 June 1916. At that time, the Steam Packet Company, which had been founded in Dublin in 1823, had four ships named after the provinces of Ireland – *Ulster, Munster, Leinster* and *Connaught*. It held the Irish Mail Contract and each ship had sorting offices on board with workers from the Dublin Post Office. However, after the start of the First World War, the *Connaught* was taken over by the British Government in 1915 and put into service as a troop carrier. Unfortunately, in 1917 the ship was torpedoed and sunk in the English Channel. During the war, the other three ships continued to operate a ferry service between England and Ireland. However, on 10 October 1918, RMS *Leinster* was also torpedoed sixteen miles out from Kingstown and sank with the loss of 501 lives. Following the war, the City of Dublin Steam Packet Company struggled mainly because of the loss of the two ships and in 1920; the Irish Mail Contract was awarded to the London and North Western Railway Company.

Left: Dublin Docks *c.*1950. A young man has a quiet smoke while sitting on a London, Midland & Southern trailer advertising Fry's Cocoa. Fry mixed cocoa powder with extracted cocoa butter to make the first eating chocolate in 1847. In Dublin, the Fry-Cadbury factory was on the Malahide Road.

Opposite below: Amiens Street *c.*1907. The street connected Memorial Road to the North Strand. The tram has just passed under the overhead railway bridge, which opened in 1891 to carry the railway loop line from Amiens Street to Westland Row. For many years the Dublin City Morgue was at numbers 2 to 4 Amiens Street.

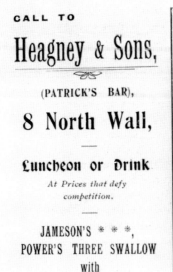

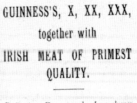

CALL TO

Heagney & Sons,

(PATRICK'S BAR),

8 North Wall,

Luncheon or Drink

At Prices that defy
competition.

JAMESON'S * * *,
POWER'S THREE SWALLOW
with

GUINNESS'S, X, XX, XXX,

together with

IRISH MEAT OF PRIMEST
QUALITY.

Private Bar and Luncheon
Room connected, with select
Bar and Sitting Room for con-
venience of all customers.

NO EXTRA CHARGE.

PREMISES LIGHTED BY
ELECTRICITY.

'PHONE 3682.

Telegraphic address—
" Heagney, Dublin."

Bed and Breakfast 3/- including attendance.   Special terms for weekly boarders.
Hot and Cold Baths 6d. extra.   No extra charge for use of sitting room and piano.

Above: Advertising card for Heagney & Sons (Patrick's Bar) public house, 8 North Wall, Dublin, *c.*1910. The premises had electric light and a telephone. They served Guinness stout and prime quality Irish meat. Guests paid three shillings (fifteen pence today) for bed and breakfast, but had to pay an extra sixpence if they wanted hot and cold baths. However, guests did have the use of the sitting room and could play the piano without charge.

The Great Northern Railway terminus, Amiens Street, *c*.1908. The station was designed by William Dean Butler and completed in 1846, costing around £7,000 in total. The imposing station was in a typically Italian style. The building was 140 feet long with a campanile or bell-tower at the centre, which was ninety feet high and smaller campaniles at each end, which were fifty-six feet in height. It was renamed Connolly Station in 1966 to honour James Connolly a prominent leader in the 1916 uprising. James Joyce, in *Ulysses* described Buck Mulligan, Stephen Daedalus and the medical students alighting from the train at Amiens Street Station to visit nearby Monto, which was then Dublin's red light district.

The Gresham Hotel, Upper Sackville Street (now O'Connell Street), *c*.1905. Thomas Gresham was an orphan who came to Dublin from London. He worked as a butler for a wealthy family in Rutland Square. However, in 1817 he purchased two town houses at 21-22 Sackville Street and started a hotel business. In 1820, number twenty also became part of the hotel. The hotel prospered, made various alterations and improvements and built up a worldwide reputation. The building survived intact during the bombardment of O'Connell Street in the 1916 Rebellion, but was totally destroyed during the Civil War in 1922, when it was occupied by the irregulars, under the command of Cathal Brugha. Following this, the hotel was rebuilt and the new Gresham Hotel opened on 16 April 1927. It has continued to attract many guests including royalty, film stars and world leaders.

A group photograph of the management and staff of the Gresham Hotel taken in 1895. At that time, the Gresham was a popular hotel for members of the Irish Home Rule Party, who would stay there in significant numbers. Their leader, John Redmond (1856-1918), always stayed at the Gresham. On the opposite side of the street were the headquarters of the United Irish League.

The Rotunda Hospital, Dublin, c.1905. The hospital was established in 1745 by Dr Bartholomew Mosse, who raised the money by private subscription and public lottery. It was built for the poor and was the first maternity hospital of its kind in these Isles. It was designed by Richard Cassels and opened in 1757. It has a very fine chapel with superb plasterwork by a Frenchman, Bartholomew Cramillion. The hospital greatly improved mortality rates for mothers and babies and soon became known for its excellent results. For over 250 years it has looked after the maternity needs of many women, particularly those living on the north side of Dublin.

The Rotunda Hospital had a worldwide reputation. The photo shows doctors at a conference at the hospital in October 1894. Front Row: A. Percival (Edinburgh Univ.), D. Lours (Univ. of Athens), W.J. Smyly (Master), E. H. Tweedy (Assist. Master), T.H. Wilson (Assist. Master), J. Murphy, (C.C.), J. Egan (Harvard). Back Row: H. Johnston (T.C.D.), F. Wynne (T.C.D.), J. Shannon (Liverpool Univ.), J. Gornall (Cambridge Univ.), H. Rutherford (T.C.D.), A. Newell (Glasgow Univ.), L. Glover (Barts), W. Winckworth (Westminster Hosp.), R. Hunter, Glasgow, A. Bill (St. Mary's Hosp.), W. Madden (Harvard), J. Dowling (Harvard), C. Swan (Harvard), H. Hewllett Hayes (Cambridge Univ.).

Gardiner Place c.1910. This road between Great Denmark Street and Mountjoy Square had fine terraced Georgian houses, which over the years became neglected and reduced to tenements. On the right of the picture stands a group of children in front of the Glenmore Private Hotel at 35 Gardiner Place. For a time James Larkin lived with his sister, Delia, at 17 Gardiner Place and Michael Collins is said to have had one of his many hiding places at the Nurses Home run by Linda Kearns in Gardiner Place.

UPPER SCHOOL SISTERS OF CHARITY, GARDINER STREET.

Young girls sit attentively on hard wooden benches at the Upper School, Sisters of Charity Convent, Upper Gardiner Street. In 1846, the Dublin Roman Catholic Archdiocese report stated that the Prioress was Mrs. Walsh and that the school had 14 religious staff and 300 poor children. The school was well known in Dublin and had a good reputation although the disciplinary regime would not be tolerated today. James Joyce in *Ulysses*, Chapter 10, describes how 'Simon Dedalus's children Katey, Boody and Maggy lunch on pea soup at the Sisters of Charity Convent on Gardiner Street'.

Hardwicke Street, showing grand Georgian houses *c.*1920. In the centre is St George's Church, which was designed by the architect Francis Johnston, who also designed the GPO. This impressive church was built around 1802 and took seven years to complete. It has a classical front façade with a portico of four fluted ionic columns and a tall sixty metre spire, which was modelled on Gibb's design for St Martin's-in-the-Fields in London. The church had a central position among the Georgian terraces and many architects consider it to be one of the finest buildings in Dublin. However, developers did not have the same opinion and unfortunately demolished many houses in the surrounding streets. The numbers in the church congregation declined and St George's was closed in the late 1980s.

St. Brigid's Workroom, 35 Belvedere Place, Dublin

Above: St Brigid's Workrooms at 35 Belvedere Place, Dublin. The young ladies are supervised as they work hard on their treadle sewing machines making vestments for the clergy.

Left: The original Abbey Theatre, Marlborough Street, Dublin, which was built partly on the site of an old morgue. The Irish National Theatre Society opened the Abbey on 27 December 1904. Dubliners enthusiastically supported the theatre, which played a major part in promoting native actors and giving a voice to Irish dramatists. The photograph for the Irish Tourist Association was taken in June 1949 and it shows semicircular roofing overhanging the entrance, which had replaced the original gabled canopy. The two plays advertised on the hoardings are *The Dreaming of the Bones* by W. B. Yeats and *The Country Dressmaker* by George Fitzmaurice. Unfortunately, this building was burnt down on 18 July 1951. The company then moved to the Queen's Theatre in Pearse Street and remained there until the new Abbey Theatre, designed by Michael Scott, opened on a larger site in Marlborough Street in 1966.

When the Abbey Theatre opened on Tuesday, 27 December, 1904, the first plays performed were *On Baile's Strand* by W. B. Yeats and the comedy *Spreading the News* by Lady Gregory. The scene shown on this postcard is from Lady Gregory's play with many of the cast on stage. Sara Allgood, standing in the centre, was born in Dublin in 1883 and raised in a Dublin orphanage. She had a distinguished career as an actress touring in Europe, Australia and New Zealand before going to America. She appeared in Hitchcock's first talking film, *Blackmail* in 1929, and in his *Juno and the Paycock* in 1930 (titled in America as *The Sins of Mary Boyle*). However, she died penniless at Woodland Hills in California in September 1950.

A group of actors *c.*1925, who performed a dramatic sketch called *Good for Nothing* at the Hibernian Hall in Rutland Square in aid of the Christian Brothers' Schools, North Brunswick Street. Back Row, from left to right: F. Bridgeman, A. O'Neil, J. Moran. Front Row: T. Morgan, Miss M. Kavanagh, Mr. J. Dolan (Instructor), J. Breen.

O'Connell Street in June 1906. Running northwards from the river, this is the best known of Dublin's wide streets with an illustrious history. The postcard shows two ladies sitting on a jaunting car. This was also called a side-car as the passengers faced the pavement with their feet resting on the footboards. Apart from a blanket they had little protection from the elements, especially the 'soft' Dublin rain. The open-topped tram, on the right, advertises Tyler's boots, which were manufactured at the factory in Marlborough Street.

The Richmond Surgical Hospital, North Brunswick Street c.1905. The hospital, built in red-brick, was founded in 1811. On the same site were the Hardwicke Fever Hospital, founded in 1803, and the Whitworth Medical Hospital, founded in 1817. Together they formed St Laurence's Hospital.

A typical ward (No. 3) at the Richmond Hospital, Dublin in 1905. It was very clean with plenty of nursing staff. There were no curtains around the beds and the only heating was provided by the coal fire in the centre of the ward. However, for those patients who were not confined to bed, the fire was the gathering point in the ward and a place for a smoke and great conversation, which itself was often therapeutic. How things have changed today!

two

Broadstone, Phoenix Park, Cabra and Phibsborough

Broadstone Terminus, Dublin, May 1911. The postcard shows a group of fashionable gentlemen on the newly delivered Connemara Touring Coach for the Midland Great Western Railway Ireland. The coach still displays an early Bedfordshire reg. no. BM 9 B and this was possibly one of the inaugural trips for demonstration purposes. The charabanc was built in Luton and supplied by Archers of Dublin. It had fifteen seats and was painted dark green with gold lettering. As there was no rail line between Clifden and Westport, the MGWR Company bought three of these coaches, which were used to carry passengers from the railway station at Clifden to Westport.

Broadstone Station, Phibsborough Road, c.1940. This imposing classical building was designed by John Skipton Mulvaney with an Egyptian style granite front and was completed in 1851. It was the terminus of the Midland Great Western Railway. However, in January 1937, the station was closed and train services were diverted to Amiens Street Station and then on to Westland Row. Coaches are shown outside the station as Broadstone remained open as a locomotive depot until 1957.

North of the Liffey, the magnificent Phoenix Park is one of the chief beauty spots of Dublin. The park covers 1,752 acres and is seven miles in circumference. It was enclosed in 1662, when a herd of fallow deer was introduced into the park by the Duke of Ormonde. Lord Chesterfield improved the park and in 1747 opened it to the public. This picture, from 1905, shows the main entrance to the park from the Quays, at the end of Parkgate Street. There are four circular limestone piers and three gates. The gates were removed for the Eucharistic Congress in 1932.

Phoenix Park, *c.*1940. The park was a popular destination for Dubliners. The postcard shows a busy scene on the main road through the park with motorists, cyclists and pedestrians all enjoying an afternoon out. The road runs for three miles in a straight line from Parkgate to Castleknock Gate. On the right is the Wellington Monument, which was erected in1861 to commemorate the victories of Dubliner Arthur Wellesley, Duke of Wellington, particularly over Napoleon Bonaparte and the French at Waterloo.

The Phoenix Column, c.1905. This was erected in 1747 by Lord Chesterfield and sited on the main road in a central position between the Parkgate and Castleknock gates. It has the mythical phoenix on top of a fluted Corinthian column, which is thirty feet high. It became a popular meeting point in the park and was also a place for the jaunting cars to turn. In the 1930s, the park became a very successful venue for motor racing and the monument was moved on safety grounds. However, it was restored to near the original position on the main road in January 1990.

A group of men, possibly a cycling club, pose for the camera at the Phoenix Column c.1930. When the Irish Government wanted to build Dublin's first airport they approached the Royal Dutch Airline, which was the world's oldest airline, for advice. They told the government that the Phoenix Park would be an ideal site for the new airport because of its open space and central location. Fortunately, this advice was rejected as it would undoubtedly have changed forever the unique character of this great park.

Spectators at a polo match in the Phoenix Park, *c.*1910. Often teams from the cavalry regiments would compete. Dubliners visited the park at weekends as they could watch many sports without charge, including polo, football, cricket and hurling. They could also enjoy the extensive parklands, admire the deer or visit the zoo.

Sunday afternoon, *c.*1909. Crowds gather to listen to a brass band playing on the bandstand in the Hollow, which was near the main entrance to the zoo. Various bands played there in turn including the St. James Brass and Reed Band, the York Street Band, the Father Mathew Band and the Catholic Boy's Brigade Band from Church Street. The Dublin United Tramways Company sponsored the bands and paid them about £4 for each performance at the Hollow. The bands attracted large crowds to the park and this brought good business to the Tramways Company.

The Vice-Regal Lodge, Phoenix Park, c.1895. This was built in 1751 for the private residence of Nathaniel Clements, Chief Ranger of the park. In 1782, the house was purchased by Nathaniel Clement's son, Robert, as a residence for the Viceroys. The wings and the columnar entrance, designed by Francis Johnston, were added in 1816. After the 1922 Treaty, Mr Tim Healy was appointed Governor General of the Irish Free State and he took up residence there on 6 December 1922. From 1938, when Douglas Hyde became President, the Lodge or 'Aras an Uachtarain' became the official residence of the President of Ireland.

House party at the Vice-Regal Lodge, Phoenix Park in April 1904. King Edward VII stands by the pillar on the right of the centre group. Royal visitors to Ireland would usually stay at the Vice-Regal Lodge and its occupants have included George IV, Queen Victoria, Edward VII and George V.

Phoenix Park Races, April 1904. On the top step from left to right: The Duke of Connaught, the Duke of Devonshire, the Marquis of Londonderry, King Edward V11 and the Lord Lieutenant.

The Phoenix Park Race Course was a popular venue for Dubliners with flat racing being held on many Saturdays in the Summer months. The photo shows Ballaghtobin, owned by Lord Decies and ridden by W. Barrett, being led in to the winners' enclosure after coming first in the Loder Plate at the Phoenix Park races in 1914. The racecourse opened in 1902 and was at the height of its popularity in the 1950s. However, after various financial problems the racecourse was closed in 1990.

The entrance to the Zoological Gardens in the Phoenix Park, c.1905. Dubliners were admitted for the first time on 1 September 1831, making this one of Europe's oldest zoos. The thatched front gate lodge was built in 1832. The superb landscaping was by the gardener, Decimus Burton. The zoo was renowned for its very successful breeding programme for lions. One of the lions became famous as the roaring lion, which introduced films from the Metro Goldwyn Meyer film studios. Dublin was also the first zoo in Europe to breed Himalayan bears.

Dublin Zoo c.1910. The postcard shows interested spectators and a giraffe with a Sudanese attendant. The zoo has always had a very good reputation and today animal welfare, breeding and the protection of endangered species remain a priority.

Dublin Zoo *c.*1950. Children stand very close, looking in awe at the large Indian elephant, Sara (1932-62), who was the last elephant used to give rides for children, and the smaller Ceylonese elephant Komali. The building on the right is the Elephant House or 'Albert Tower', which was built in 1845-6 to house a giraffe. On the death of the giraffe the elephants moved into the house. It was designed by George Wilkinson, who was also the architect for Harcourt Street Station.

Dublin Zoo *c.*1910. The postcard shows the keeper casually smoking a cigarette as he strokes the Duchess of Connaught's panther. Would health and safety approve? The zoo has had two deaths when animals attacked their keepers. The first was in 1880, when an Irish reindeer attacked and killed a keeper who was cleaning out its stable. After this incident the reindeer's antlers were removed. The second death was in 1883 when an elephant named Tito crushed its keeper's head under a foot. It was decided that the elephant was dangerous and it was destroyed by a firing party from the Royal Irish Constabulary.

The Royal Hibernian Military School near the Chapelizod entrance in Phoenix Park was established by the Hibernian Society in 1768 to serve as an orphanage to save unfortunate children from poverty. For many years, lay teachers conducted the school, but they were eventually replaced by teachers from the military. The children were usually the sons and daughters of soldiers. Many of the boys would join the army themselves. The postcard shows the staff of the Military School and some students from the Training College in 1916.

Prize Day at the Royal Hibernian Military School in 1916. Major-General Maxwell, the Commander-in-Chief of the Forces in Ireland and the Vice-President of the School, is shown inspecting the boys who are smartly dressed in their uniforms. Following the Easter Rising, Maxwell was responsible for confirming the execution of fifteen of the rebel leaders and also imposing martial law. These acts caused public outrage and the effect of the executions was to make martyrs of the rebels.

A boy's race at Royal Hibernian Military School in Summer 1920. The British army military instructor (second from the right) wears World War 1 medal ribbons.

Dragoon horse guards on parade at Marlborough Barracks, Phoenix Park, *c*.1910. The cavalry barracks were built in 1892 on Blackhorse Avenue. The building is imposing and resembles a French Chateau with its red brick and terracotta turrets and steep roofs. Over 800 horses were kept in the stables. They were renamed as McKee Barracks in honour of Brigadier Richard McKee, who was killed at Croke Park on Bloody Sunday in 1920.

Arch: Hamilton Rowan

Rowan Hamilton (1805-65) was a child prodigy and a brilliant mathematician who studied at Trinity College, Dublin and was appointed Professor of Astronomy at the university in 1827, even before he graduated. He became a friend of Wordsworth, but his talents were in science and not poetry. In 1843, he discovered that geometrical operations in three dimensions required a fourth dimension for the purpose of calculation. This solution is said to have occurred to him while walking along the Royal Canal at Cabra with his wife. He promptly carved the formulae for the quaternion on the stonework of Brougham Bridge at Cabra.

The school parade at St. Joseph's, Cabra, c.1910. This was the Catholic Institution for the Deaf and Dumb, run by the Christian Brothers, which gained an international reputation for its teaching. Notable past pupils include the Irish soccer international, Peter Desmond and the Gaelic footballer, Thomas Gallagher, who won an All-Ireland Championship Medal playing for Mayo.

The Dominican Convent, Cabra. The former mansion of the Segrave family who had a distinguished member, Sir Henry Segrave, who died aged thirty-four on 13 June 1930 trying to set a new world record for water-speed on Lake Windermere. The house with twelve acres of land was purchased by the nuns in 1819. They ran a school for the poor children of Cabra for some years and then, with the support of the Archbishop of Dublin, they opened a boarding school in 1835. The convent thrived and a superb chapel was built in 1851. Over the years the convent was very successful and further expansion took place. St Gabriel's School for Deaf Girls was opened on the site. The chapel was enlarged in 1905.

A happy group of girls from the third year at the Dominican Convent, Cabra in March 1946. Back row: Ruth Russell, Eleanor, Margaret and Pat. Front row: Agatha, Angela and Tony.

St Peter's Chapel and Free Schools, Phibsborough, *c*.1850, drawn by George Petrie, RHA. The Chapel was built of limestone and stood at the junction of Cabra Avenue and the North Circular Road. Beneath the chapel steps was the free-school where poor children from the district were educated.

Phibsborough crossroads and Doyle's Corner, c.1940, showing St Peter's Church in the centre. The church was designed by George Goldie in the early Gothic style in 1869. The initial director of the project was Father McNamara, who was a co-founder of St Joseph's School for Deaf Boys, Cabra and who also founded All Hallows College, Drumcondra. However, there were planning problems and the magnificent church and two-hundred foot spire was not fully completed until 1911.

The Mater Hospital, designed by John Bourke, opened in 1861. It was run by the Sisters of Mercy founded by Catherine McAuley. For many years, until Beaumount Hospital opened, it was the main centre of treatment for the north side of the city. In *Ulysses*, Leopold Bloom, who lived down the road at No. 7 Eccles Street, went to the Mater Hospital for treatment after a bee sting. The growth of the hospital over many years has led to the destruction of some of the original Georgian architecture in the area.

The Children's Hospital, Temple Street. The hospital was established in 1872 to aid the poor children of Dublin. It was run by the Sisters of Charity for a hundred years before coming under the care of the Sisters of Mercy. This card was posted in December 1909. It was written to Mr. J.P. Woodhead, Scoutmaster of the First Phoenix Park Boy Scout Troup telling him that his boys will be most welcome in the wards on Christmas Eve to distribute toys to the little patients.

The Dominican College, 15-17 Eccles Street – Junior girls' class, 1914.

The Dominican College, 15-17 Eccles Street – Junior boys' class, 1914.

Dominican College, 15-17 Eccles Street, Dublin. Girl's First Communion Class 1950. Rev. Father Campbell sits in the centre.

Dominican College, 15-17 Eccles Street, Dublin. Girl's First Communion Class, May 1953. Front Row: K. Bourke, P. McManus, M. Farrell, A. Malone, M. Morgan, M. Breslin, J. O'Reilly, G. O'Hara, V. Poole. Second Row: E. Burke, C. Hussey, M. O'Kennedy, C. Farrell, Rev. Fr. E. Hayden, O. P., M. Hayward, G. Grogan, M. Caffrey, J. Archer.
Third Row: Y. Morton, J. Lenehan, F. Devine, J. Stritch, B. McCabe, M. O'Reilly, N. Flinter, A. Warren, F. McGivern, D. Callanan, P. Donelan.

Cross Guns Bridge. Dublin

A tram is shown crossing the Westmoreland Bridge, known as Cross Guns Bridge. The entrance to the Dublin North City Milling Company is on the left. The bridge was built in 1791 by the Royal Canal Company. It was modernised and widened in 1912 and was 'hump-backed' before being levelled in the late 1920s. In the nineteenth century the fields by the bridge were a duelling ground and this is the likely reason for the name of the bridge. On 26 December 1826, there was a famous duel at the bridge when John Bric, who supported Daniel O'Connell, was shot dead by William Hayes, a Conservative from Cork.

The Dublin North City Milling Co. Ltd., 113 Phibsborough Road, Dublin. c.1932. The installation of new machinery for flour milling by MIAG of Brunswick Germany was taking place, as hoisting apparatus is noticeable under the windows in the yard. The man with the briefcase was a German engineer. Milling had taken place on this site since 1860. Barges on the canal were used for transport. The mill came under the ownership of Ranks Ireland Ltd. in 1953.

three

Finglas, Glasnevin and Drumcondra

The start of the non-stop Motor Cycle race from Tolka Bridge, Dublin to Dundalk, *c*.1905. The Motor Cycle Union of Ireland resulted from a meeting called by the Dublin motorcyclist and publisher James Percy held on 7 March 1902, at the Metropole Hotel, Dublin. The first president was John Boyd Dunlop, inventor of the pneumatic tyre. The first social run was from Phoenix Park to Bray on 26 April 1902. An Ulster group was started in Belfast in January 1903 and the two groups would meet occasionally in Dundalk to discuss any problems.

Finglas Village and St Canice's Church *c*.1950. Finglas, or Fionnghlas, means 'pure stream' and takes its name from a small river tributary, which used to flow through the village. The writer of the card, on holiday from Lincoln in England, says that 'talk about living in the country – it couldn't be much better than here'. However, as inner city tenements were demolished, new houses were needed for those who had lost their homes. Large housing estates were built around Dublin. During the 1960s Finglas was developed for housing and this totally changed the rural suburb.

Montgomery & Sons Butcher's Shop, Main Road, Finglas in 1937. A fine selection of meat on display. Even the local telegraph pole is brought into service.

Joseph Montgomery, Commissioner, making presentations to young scouts at Finglas in 1937. Tom Montgomery is also in the group. The scouting movement, which encouraged open air life and social responsibility, was very popular and at that time there were many Boy Scout troops in Dublin.

A happy group of guests gather in the back garden at 9 Botanic Avenue, Glasnevin following the wedding of May Elizabeth Montgomery to Edward John Kane on 19 August 1946. Back Row (from left to right): James M., Pansy Lawless (former Royalette at the Theatre Royal), Christopher Kane. Front Row: Harry Montgomery, Marion Lawless, -?- , Celestine Montgomery, Irene Kane, Edward John Kane, May Elizabeth Montgomery, Celestine Montgomery (junior), Joseph Montgomery, Rev. Fr. Furlong (Parish Priest of Our Lady of Dolours Church, Glasnevin), John Montgomery.

Glasnevin Cemetery, Dublin. In September 1831, the land had been bought by the Burial Committee of the Catholic Association and was at first called Prospect Cemetery. It was surrounded by high walls with watchtowers from where a look out could be kept for body-snatchers. In the centre of the picture is Parnell's grave. The Chapel, which is similar in design to Cormac's Chapel on the Rock of Cashel, is on the right. The Round Tower rises above the vault containing the coffin of Daniel O'Connell, Ireland's 'Liberator' from the penal laws, who in his last moments bequeathed his 'soul to heaven, his heart to Rome, and his body to Ireland'.

Mourners at the grave of Charles Stewart Parnell at Glasnevin Cemetery. Parnell was one of Ireland's greatest leaders and, but for the scandal in 1890, when he was named as co-respondent in the divorce case of Captain William O'Shea, he may well have achieved Home Rule for Ireland. After marrying Kitty O'Shea, he died in Brighton, England the following year. His body was brought back to Dublin and many thousands attended his funeral at Glasnevin on Sunday, 11 October 1891.

The burial of President Arthur Griffiths, the founder of Sinn Fein, at Glasnevin on 12 August 1922. Michael Collins is seen on the left of the photograph – he too was to die in an ambush, at Beal na Blath in County Cork, ten days later on 22 August 1922. His body was brought back to Dublin for a state funeral. Thousands of mourners lined the streets as his coffin was transported on a gun carriage drawn by four black horses to Glasnevin, where he was buried on the right of the main entrance gate.

Mourners looking at the floral tributes at the grave of Kevin O'Higgins at Glasnevin Cemetery in July 1927. O'Higgins, as Minister for Home Affairs, was a strongman of the first Irish Free State Government. He was instrumental in the establishment of the Garda Siochana. He was shot dead on 10 July 1927 by fringe Irish Republicans, as he made his way to mass at Booterstown. As he lay dying he repeatedly forgave his murderers.

Above: The Botanic Gardens, Glasnevin, *c.*1890s. These were originally the lands surrounding the house of Addison, the eighteenth century essayist. Fifty acres of the land was purchased in 1793 from the family of the poet, Thomas Tickle, by the Dublin (later Royal Dublin) Society to establish the gardens. Many generations of Dubliners have enjoyed walking in the gardens. The Tolka River flows through the gardens, which include beautiful flower beds, shrubberies, rockeries, water gardens and large Victorian glasshouses with rare and exotic plants. The Great Palm-House was built in 1884. The collection of orchids is recognised as one of the finest in the world. There is a fine yew walk, which is still known as 'Addison's Walk'.

Opposite below: The First Communion Class at Scoil Mhuire Christian Brothers' School, Griffith Avenue, Marino, Easter 1931.

Above: The Committee and friends of the Glasnevin Football Club on their annual outing gather at the entrance to the Botanic Gardens in 1954. Included in the photo are Tommy Irwin, Carl Connon, Danny O'Brien, Michael Kelly, Joseph Montgomery, Gerry Connon, Gus O'Connor, Michael McCarthy, Percy Mulligan and Peter Gaffney.

The First Communion Class in 1954 at the Holy Faith School, Iona, Glasnevin.

St. Patrick's College, Drumcondra, Dublin.

Students in the grounds of St Patrick's College, Drumcondra, *c*.1910. This was the training college for Catholic male teachers under the patronage of the Archbishop of Dublin. It was established in 1785 and stayed at Nos. 1 and 2 Drumcondra Road until 1883, before moving to its present site at Belvedere House.

Multi-view of St Patrick's National Schools, Drumcondra on a postcard dated 15 August 1905. The sender of the card, a teacher who trained at St. Patrick's College, says 'this is the place where we had to serve our apprenticeship to the pedagogic part of our programme. We had great fun during our time here.'

Holy Cross College, looking north, Clonliffe, Dublin. Clonliffe was originally the site of St Mary's Abbey, which was founded by Benedictine monks from Savigny c.1140. Clonliffe House was purchased by Paul Cardinal Cullen, Archbishop of Dublin, in 1858. Holy Cross College was opened as a seminary for the Dublin Diocese on 18 May, 1863.

Upper Drumcondra Road, c.1910. A child stands outside the newsagent and tobacconist. At that time, local shops performed a vital service for the community. There were no supermarkets and the corner shop would stock newspapers, foods, drinks, tobacco and sweets of all kinds, including sherbet, liquorice, aniseed balls and lollipops.

Ferguson Road, Drumcondra, with neat rows of semi-detached houses c.1940. An omnibus runs down the road heading for the city. In the 1930s there were many pirate buses, but by the 1940s, there were just three main bus companies. These were The Great Northern, The Great Southern and Dublin United Tramways.

four

Artane, Killester, Clontarf and Dollymount

Left: The Irish postcard artist, John Carey, depicts Brian Boru, at the Battle of Clontarf, on Good Friday, 23 April 1014. At that time, Dublin was ruled by the Danish leader, Sitric. The Irish forces under Brian Boru advanced from Drumcondra and the Danes of Dublin had a front extending from the city to the mouth of the river Tolka at Fairview. The battle, which was very fierce, lasted from dawn to sunset and resulted in a very heavy defeat for the Danish forces. However, both sides lost most of their leaders in the fighting. Unfortunately, Brian Boru, while alone in his tent giving thanks for the victory, was attacked and killed by Brodir, a Viking leader who was fleeing from the battle. This meant that three generations of the ruling Irish family had died in the battle - Brian, his son Murrough and his grandson Turlough. However, Danish power in Ireland was ended once and for all.

Below: Confirmation Class at Scoil Mhuire Christian Brothers School, Griffith Avenue, Marino in 1946. The boys look very smart and all proudly wear their rosettes and medals.

Fairview Corner, Dublin, *c.*1940. In 1912, the shops at the corner were Hayes, Coningham and Robinson, pharmaceutical chemists and William Lewis, a grocer and provision merchant. The shop on the far right has an advertisement for Fry's chocolate.

A quiet scene at Killester shops, *c.*1945. The bus driver and conductor are taking a break. Scott's delivery van is outside Egan's shop. The shop on the right is H. S. Kincaid.

The Confirmation Class at St Brigid's National School, Killester in 1963.

This eighteenth century house at Dollymount, called Thornhill was purchased by the brothers Arthur and Benjamin Guinness in 1835. It was renamed St Anne's, probably from an ancient holy well on the estate. The house remained in the Guinness family. In 1880, Arthur Edward Guinness was made a peer and became Lord Ardilaun. He developed the house and estate and had a driveway lain, which was one and a half miles long, to the Howth Road. At the time of his death in 1904, the estate covered 460 acres. However, the house was vandalized during the 1960s and had to be demolished in 1968.

Marino Crescent, Clontarf, c.1907. This fine Georgian crescent of houses which had great views of Dublin Bay was built in 1792. The Crescent connected Malahide Road and Howth Road. It is well known as the birthplace of Bram Stoker (1847-1912), the author of *Dracula*. He was born at number 15 Marino Crescent on 8 November 1847. He went to Trinity College where he excelled at athletics and after graduation joined the civil service. However, he loved the theatre and soon left the civil service to work as secretary to the great actor, Sir Henry Irving, who was said to have an overpowering personality. It is likely that Stoker based his Dracula character on Irving and today Count Dracula, the vampire, is well known throughout the world.

The tree-lined St Lawrence Road, running from Howth Road to Clontarf Road. This road to the sea is one of the green lanes of Clontarf, well known for their fine houses and sylvan beauty. It is no surprise that Dillon Cosgrave in his book on North Dublin in 1909 describes the areas of Clontarf and Howth as having the pleasant distinction of possessing the lowest death rates in the neighbourhood of Dublin.

The Great North Wall, more popularly known as the Bull Wall, at Dollymount was built between 1800 and 1825 to help maintain a deep channel to Dublin Port. The clockwise movement of the tidal currents in Dublin Bay then led to the deposition of sand, forming Bull Island, which is still slowly growing towards Sutton shore. The sand dunes are a great recreational area for Dubliners, but are also a very important nature reserve and bird sanctuary.

The Royal Dublin Golf Club House, Dollymount, erected in 1904. The golf shop to the left of the pavilion was run by Tom Hood who was the professional at the club from 1896 to 1914. The Golf Club was formed in May 1885 at a meeting held at 19 Grafton Street. It was initially located in the Phoenix Park, but moved to the links course at Bull Island in 1889. Unfortunately, on the night of 2 August 1943, the clubhouse was gutted by fire. However, a new clubhouse was eventually completed in October 1954. Christy O'Connor was appointed club professional in 1959 and his international success enhanced the reputation of the Royal Dublin Golf Club.

five

Sutton and Howth

An early photograph of Howth Village and Ireland's Eye, *c.*1885. The Martello Tower is on the right and the Catholic Church of the Assumption is not yet built. In 1805, Howth was selected as the best place for a storm harbour and packet station for Dublin. Work commenced in 1807 with the construction of the East Pier. The West Pier was started in 1810. On 1 August 1818, Howth became the mail station for Dublin. At that time, the journey from Holyhead to Howth by sailing ship took around fifteen hours. When steam packet boats were introduced in 1822, the journey was reduced to around six hours. Unfortunately, the harbour was continually silting up with sand, so that large vessels could not dock in safety. This problem had been foreseen during construction and the project has been described as the greatest engineering fiasco in Ireland's history. The main engineer, John Rennie, is said to have committed suicide. Therefore, in view of the problems with Howth Harbour, Dun Laoghaire was made the packet station for Dublin in 1834.

The Dublin train from Howth steams into Sutton Railway Station, *c.*1907. There were superb views from the train as it ran along the coast. Passengers wait on the station platform which would certainly be more crowded today. The wall on the opposite platform carries advertisements, including one for 'Wrights Coal Tar Soap'.

Sutton Cross *c*.1950. The G.N.R. Hill of Howth Tram (No. 1), shown on the return journey from Howth to Sutton. The large white building in the centre of the photograph is the Sutton Cinema. When the cinema closed the building was taken over by Superquinn. The schoolchildren on the right are waiting at the bus stop, which is outside the Marine Hotel.

Trams at Sutton Station ready to go to Howth Summit. In good weather, especially at weekends, a ride on the Howth Tram to the summit would be a very popular trip out for the family. Here the first tramcar (No. 9) is full and the driver has placed a sign in the front window saying 'Car to follow'.

Hill of Howth Tram (No. 2) at Howth Terminus *c*.1950. The entrance to the railway station is on the right. The railway photographer, W.A. ('Cam') Camwell is shown on the left carrying a case. Also in the distance to the left of the railway signal cabin is the Claremount Hotel (see page 63).

Howth Station, *c*.1950. Train No. 188 stands at the platform with the Hill of Howth Tram (No. 2) on the right. It was very convenient for the passengers as they would leave the train and then board the tram outside the station. The tram would then leave the station by taking the track on the right and climbing rapidly up the hill.

A popular postcard *c*.1940, which shows the No. 8 tram leaving Howth Station and ascending the hill to the summit with Ireland's Eye in the background. The traction poles are on the right of the line. The passengers had superb panoramic views across Dublin Bay of the city and coastline, with the Dublin and Wicklow mountains behind.

Unfortunately, the Hill of Howth tram line closed on 14 May 1959. This photograph, taken on Station Road beside Sutton Railway Station, shows the No. 1 tram near the end of its service. On the right are the conductor Paddy O'Dowd, who is in uniform and Tom Redmond, senior motorman, known as 'The Colonel'. The girl in the centre of the picture is Bridie McKenny McMorrow and the man with the camera is her husband Jimmy McMorrow. The lady on his left is Josie Shields. It was on 31 May 1959, seen off by Lord and Lady Howth and the Saint Lawrence Pipe Band that the No. 1 tram, driven by Tom Redmond, made the last trip up the hill.

Passengers boarding the Howth tram (No. 307) for Dublin at the East Pier terminus, *c.*1905. This tram was built in Preston in 1900 and had seats for thirty people on the lower deck and forty-five on the upper. The lower deck had curtains on the windows. The waiting room and parcels office is on the right. This was a time when trams were a very busy popular form of transport. However, during the 1930s, the Dublin trams were no longer profitable and the Dublin United Tram Company closed the line in March 1941.

A view of Howth Village *c.*1920. The Catholic Church of the Assumption is on the right with the Martello Tower on the hill behind. In the distance is Ireland's Eye. This is an island which has a long history of early Christian settlement by the three sons of Nessan from the Royal House of Leinster. They established a church there and produced a copy of the four gospels *The Garland of Howth*, which is now in the library at Trinity College Dublin. There were Viking invasions in the tenth century and the monks transferred to St Mary's Abbey in the thirteenth century. In 1803, a Martello Tower, seen at the far left, was built on the Island.

The old village of Howth on a postcard dated 19 July 1916. The village is a quiet retreat with picturesque thatched cottages on both sides of the street. The road surface is rough. Further up the street on the left, children play on the pavement outside their houses. The rear of the Church of the Assumption is on the right.

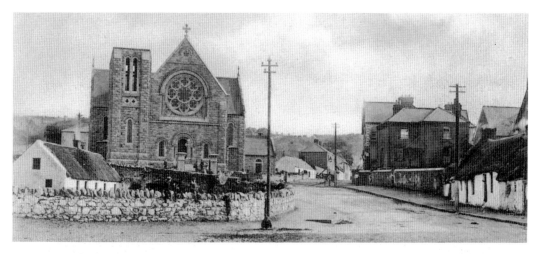

The main street in Howth showing the Church of the Assumption on a postcard dated 1905. Work commenced on the church, designed by W. H. Byrne, in 1894. However, during excavation of the site, the remains of an armoury were found. It is thought that this may have been the place where Sir Armorey Tristam's and Sir John de Courcey's Knights got ready for battle, when they landed at Howth in 1177. Tristam's victory secured him the title to the Lands of Howth and he became the first Baron of Howth. The church was consecrated by Archbishop Walsh of Dublin on 15 October 1899. However, the tower took longer to build and the planned spire was never completed. The church bell was installed in the tower in 1906.

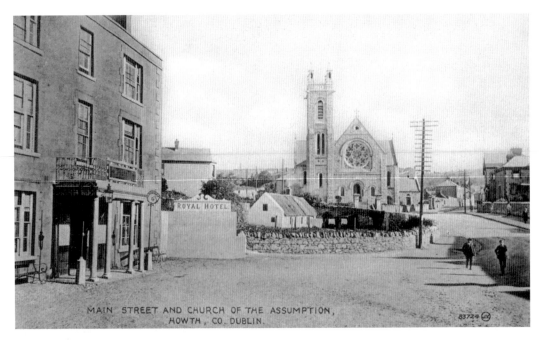

Howth Main Street, *c*.1940. The Church of the Assumption with its bell tower is in the centre. The Royal Hotel is on the left. This hotel was originally built as the Postillion Coach House and opened in the 1830s to serve passengers travelling between England and Howth on the Mail Boats. The stagecoaches from Dublin stopped here.

Main Street, Howth *c*.1940. A man and a young boy sit on the wall by the Royal Hotel. The women are admiring the babies, while their men folk watch from a distance.

Abbey Street and Church Street, Howth, Co. Dublin.

Junction of Abbey Street and Church Street, Howth *c.*1950. There was very little traffic so the children were able to ride on their homemade trolleys. The trolleys were made using old pram wheels and could certainly speed down the hill towards the harbour road.

The Claremont Hotel, Howth had spectacular views over Ireland's Eye and Lambay Island and a fine private beach at Claremont Strand. It was a popular hotel and in 1932, full board was 15 shillings a day (equivalent to 75 pence today) or 84 shillings (£4.20p) a week. Unfortunately, after several owners, it became unprofitable and today there are luxury apartments on the site.

Howth Harbour, *c.*1895. A good view of the lighthouse on the West Pier with the panorama of Dublin Bay coast in the background. An important historical event took place there on 26 July 1914, when the yacht *Asgard* owned by Erskine Childers landed 900 rifles for the use of the Dublin Battalion of the Irish Volunteers. While returning to Dublin the Volunteers were met at Clontarf by a force of British soldiers and police. However, they scattered across the fields and only about twenty guns were confiscated by the soldiers. The Dublin Battalion held the remaining weapons and many were used in 1916.

Howth Fishing Pier on a card posted on 4 September 1907, showing a visitor smoking a pipe, while inspecting the trawler, *Herbert Lfith*. Herring fishing was done at night by drift-net and the writer of the card says that he cannot go out that night to fish, as the weather is wet and rough, so he is spending the time writing and thinking.

The Fishing Fleet in Howth Harbour, *c.*1910. Howth has been an established fishing port since the ninth century. During the herring season many boats would come to fish out of Howth. The harbour would then be so crowded that it was possible to walk from pier to pier across the boats. Howth remains the second largest fishing centre in Ireland. The coal importers, Samuel Irwin and Co., are located on the quayside.

Howth Harbour on a postcard dated 14 June 1925. Two boys in school uniform walk on the harbour wall past the fishing fleet. Around then, on most days, Howth Pier was a busy place as there would always be fishermen mending nets and others salting the fresh herring or barrelling fish for market. The writer of the card describes a very pleasant day 'being on Howth Head listening to the waves lapping the cliffs'.

Howth House, c.1895. Sir Walter Herbert Boyd (1835-1918) High Court Judge and the first
Commodore of Howth Sailing Club (now Howth Yacht Club) pictured with his family at the back of
the bank. The house was on the waterfront under St. Mary's Abbey and the rear garden was very private.

A peaceful scene in the rear garden at Howth House, c.1895. The photograph shows the back of this
impressive house with the Judge relaxing on a bench in the garden. On the left, a child sits on the swing
in the shadow of the tree.

At the front of Howth House in the Croydon carriage, *c*.1890. The house was built in 1807 on the Harbour Road at the corner of Abbey Street. The resident engineer lived there when the original Harbour was built between 1807 and 1817. It was leased by Sir Walter Boyd and his family in 1875, and they later purchased the house and lived there for six months every summer, spending the winter in their town house at 66 Merrion Square.

Sir Walter Boyd sailing in Howth Harbour on his yacht *Hofda c*.1885. He was a pioneer of Howth sailing and had a number of other yachts. However, he is best known for designing the Howth seventeen-footers. These were boats for experienced sailors' with 335 square foot of sail. The initial five craft, *Leila, Rita, Silver Moon, Aura* and *Hera*, raced for the first time on 4 May 1898. Over the years more boats of the same design have been added and Howth is well known for having the oldest single design racing fleet in the world.

A postcard showing yachts sailing in Howth Harbour on a calm day *c.*1905. The East Pier with its lighthouse is on the right and the West Pier is on the left.

Howth Harbour *c.*1910, showing the lifeboat, *James Stephens* No. 7, which was a forty-five foot Watson class lifeboat. The lifeboat was in service from 1899 to 1926 and was involved in several rescues.

The Cosy Restaurant and Private Hotel, Harbour Road, Howth, *c*.1907. At that time, the proprietor was Miss Shanahan. The ladies in their long skirts have left the cycle store which is on the left next to the hotel and are preparing to take to the open road.

Members of Howth Sailing Club in competition in Summer 1939. An exciting race showing *Tinker Bell* (No. 15), with Aideen Stokes at the helm, just ahead of *Wendy* (No. 14), helmed by John Masset and *Cinder* (No. 4), with Artie Corbett at the helm.

More racing at Howth in Summer 1939 showing a close start with from left to right, the *Mermaid Minx* (No. 8) with Jimmy Mooney at the helm, the Essex One Design *Cinder 2*, helmed by George Corbett with Dermot, Luke and Peggy Corbett crewing, and the National *Tinker Bell* (No. 15) with Norman Wilkinson at the helm.

Above: Howth from the Pier, *c.*1920, showing old fishermen passing the time. On the right is Findlaters, the food and wine merchants with its familiar clock. During the early days of Howth Sailing Club, on the start of their races through the Harbour mouth, the time would be taken from Findlaters clock. Howth Yacht Club was founded in 1968 when the Sailing Club and Motor Yacht Club amalgamated.

Opposite top: The Bathing Strand at Balscadden with the East Pier and Ireland's Eye in the distance. The place name, Balscadden is a Gaelic word meaning 'Town of the Herring' and the bay was well known by Howth fishermen for having masses of herring. The changing cubicles for ladies on the strand were provided by the railway company to encourage passengers to visit Howth.

Opposite middle: Ruins of St. Mary's Abbey, Howth, *c.*1910. The first church on this cliffside site overlooking the harbour was built by Sitric, a Norse king of Dublin, in 1042. Only the Porch and Western Doorway remain of that church. The Abbey had a bell tower over the main door which held three bells. These bells would be rung at funerals. Three bells would toll for a man, two bells for a woman and one for a child.

Opposite bottom: Howth Castle. Older parts of the castle date from the fifteenth century. There are magnificent gardens with a spectacular rhododendron grove. The St. Lawrence family were Lords of Howth from 1177 to 1909, when the inheritance passed to the sister of the last Lord Howth. The family still live in the castle.

The Baily Lighthouse at Howth Head, which was constructed by George Halpin and completed in 1814. The interior of the lantern had a mosaic floor. The lighthouse was lit first with oil and then from 1865 with gas. A revolving lens, driven by a clockwork machine manually wound every thirty minutes, was installed in 1902. The lighthouse had a staff of four keepers and several assistant keepers. The Baily went automatic in 1972, when the optics were replaced with an electric bulb and a smaller lens, which was operated and powered by electricity. However, it remained manned until March 1997, when it became fully automated.

K. B. S. group Howth, 1925. The girl fourth from the right in the third row is Marjorie Barrett (*neé* Henry).

six

People and Events

The St. Laurence O'Toole Pipe Band, c.1925. This famous band was founded in 1910 with the first President being Thomas Clarke and the first Secretary Sean O'Casey. It was the official band of the Irish Volunteers and took part in the St. Patrick's Day Parade prior to Easter Week 1916. The band would also often play before All-Ireland finals at Croke Park. Shown in the group are Thomas Duffy (Pipe Sergeant), Liam Clare (Pipe Major), Laurence White (Drum Sergeant), John Maguire (President) and Thomas Hannan (Secretary). The boy to the left of the drums is Bonney from Donnycarney.

Dan O'Dowd (1903-1989), the doyen of Irish uilleann pipers, with his sons Dermot, Edmund, Liam and Rory. Born in the Liberties in Dublin, in his youth, Dan was a member of Fianna Eireann under the command of Sean McBride. This involvement led to his internment in Mountjoy Jail in the early 1920s. While there he continued to play his pipes upsetting the Governor, Paudeen O'Keefe, who had him transferred to the Curragh Camp. On his eventual release, he played his pipes as the internees marched out of Kingsbridge Station, to be greeted by Maude Gonne McBride. Dan, a close friend of Willie Clancy, had a long and distinguished career and had a great rapport with young musicians always finding time to encourage and teach them. He worked throughout his life to develop the traditional art of piping and also maintain the craft of uilleann pipe-making in Ireland.

Dan O'Dowd with the uilleann pipes playing for President Patrick and Mrs Hillery at Aras an Uachtarain in 1986. Dan died on 22 June 1989 and was buried at Balgriffin Cemetery in north County Dublin.

Mount Sackville, Chapelizod was built for Lord George Sackville around 1740. The house later became a convent and this postcard has several views of the Mount Sackville Convent, Phoenix Park *c.*1910, including the school orchestra and the junior boys' class.

Artane National School, Kilmore Road *c.*1919. The Principal, Mr. Peter Keane from Skerries, stands at the rear.

ENTRANCE, PHOENIX PARK, EUCHARISTIC CONGRESS, DUBLIN, 1932.   216342.JV.

Above: The grand entrance to the Phoenix Park specially constructed for the thirty-first Eucharistic Congress, which was held in Dublin from 22-26 June 1932. The Papal Legate, Cardinal Lorenzo Lauri arrived in the park on the Sunday to celebrate the Pontifical High Mass. He was supported by eight cardinals and hundreds of bishops representing forty-eight countries.

Opposite below: Clonmore Road, North Strand, Dublin showing houses propped up after the German bombing on Friday 31 May 1941. On that night, bombs also fell on Summerhill and in the Phoenix Park. It was the Whit weekend and people were totally unprepared for the bombing. Twenty-seven people died and forty-five people were seriously injured. The number of houses destroyed was twenty-five. The German Reich later paid compensation for the damage, claiming the bombing was an accident. However, there have been suggestions that the North Strand bombing and the bombing in Phoenix Park (possibly intended for President Douglas Hyde in Aras an Uachtarain) may have been aimed at putting pressure on the Irish Government. In April 1941, some fire engines from Dublin, Drogheda and Dundalk had been sent to Belfast to help fight fires, after German bombing in the city.

Above: Aerial View showing the High Altar and over one million people in the Phoenix Park for the Pontifical High Mass. Pilgrims had come from all over Ireland and from every corner of the world. Those attending were reminded that they should conduct themselves as if they were in church and that they should not smoke from the time they assembled in Phoenix Park until the conclusion of benediction on Watling Street Bridge. Areas in the park were designated for the men on the gospel side and the women on the epistle side of the high altar. Count John McCormack sang the Panis Angelicus at the mass. The Congress was an outstanding success bringing the people of Ireland and the world together under the common bond of the Catholic faith.

A wedding takes place at St Agatha's Church, North William Street, North Strand on 21 July 1951. The church was designed by William H. Byrne in a classical roman renaissance style and was completed in 1908. It had strong solid walls and the building survived the North Strand bombing in 1941. However, all the church windows were blown out.

MATT TALBOT

Matt Talbot was born in May 1856 at 13 Aldborough Court, Dublin. He was sent to the Christian Brothers Schools, North Richmond Street and left school at the age of twelve. His first job was as a messenger boy with the firm of Edward and John Burke, wine merchants, where he first began drinking alcohol. He had a succession of jobs which he could not hold for long and he became a confirmed alcoholic, whose life revolved around drink. However, he underwent a profound religious conversion in 1884 and became a teetotaller and ascetic. His life was a model of all that was good. As well as his work on Dublin Docks, his life included daily mass and communion, prayer, fasting and self-mortification. When he was admitted to the Mater Hospital in June 1923, he was diagnosed with heart disease and an irregular heart beat. He died suddenly in June 1925. The nuns who prepared him for burial found that he had chains around his waist, which he had worn for years. Since his death, a cult of devotion has grown around Matt Talbot with Archbishop Byrne formally starting the cause for his canonisation in 1937.

Right: The house at 18 Upper Rutland Street where Matt Talbot lived with his mother after his father died in 1899. This area and Summerhill was then in decline. However, Shaw's Directory in 1850 listed Upper Rutland Street as 'a street of solicitors and barristers'.

Below: Granby Lane, Dublin, where Matt Talbot died suddenly while on his way to St Saviour's Dominican Church on 7 June 1925. The rear of the church and priory can be seen at the end of the lane. For two years Matt Talbot had been unwell and had twice received treatment as an in-patient at the Mater hospital for an irregular heart beat. While in hospital, he had spent all his spare time in the hospital chapel and at one time was given the last rites.

Exterior of No. 18 Rutland St. Dublin where Matt Talbot resided

Granby Lane Dublin where Matt Talbot died

After his death and the circumstances of his life became widely known, devotion to Matt Talbot spread and people prayed for favours through his intercession. This shows pilgrims at Matt Talbot's grave at Glasnevin Cemetery *c*.1926.

Flight of Southern Cross from Portmarnock Beach to New York on 24 June 1913. They had waited almost three weeks for good weather. The crew who had stayed overnight at the Grand Hotel, Malahide, stand in front of the plane, from left to right: Mr. Evert Van Dyke (Asst. Pilot), Captain Paddy Saul (Navigator), Major Charles Kingsland–Smith or 'Smithy' (Pilot) and Mr. John Stannage (Radio Operator). This was only the second airplane flight across the Atlantic from East to West. The previous flight in 1928 from Baldonnel Aerodrome by two Germans in a Bremen, (Junkers monoplane), had crash landed on Greenly Island off Labrador.

Right: Alfie Byrne (1882-1956) was the longest serving Lord Mayor of Dublin with nine years of service from 1930-39 and also1954-55. He became a 'man of the people' and was popularly known as the children's Lord Mayor, as he increased the number of playgrounds in the city. He travelled everywhere by bicycle.

Below: Crowds gather on Portmarnock Beach on 18 August 1932 for the departure of *The Hearts Content* on the first solo non-stop east to west crossing of the Atlantic. Paddy Saul had assisted in charting the course. The card shows the Lord Mayor, Alfie Byrne, in morning suit, greeting the pilot, Mr. Jim Mollinson, wishing him good luck and giving him letters for delivery to prominent people in New York. At 11 a.m., the silver coloured De Havilland Puss Moth monoplane *The Hearts Content* gathered speed along the beach and took off for America. After flying for just over thirty hours, heavy headwinds forced the aircraft to land at Pennfield Ridge. The following day, Sunday 21 August the plane completed the final 600 miles to land at Roosevelt Field Aerodrome, Long Island, New York. Jim Mollison, who was called the 'British Lindbergh' received a tremendous reception.

Opposite below: Crowds, controlled by the Garda, gather on Portmarnock Beach prior to the departure of the Southern Cross for New York (via Newfoundland) at 4.30 am on Tuesday 24 June 1913. The aircraft had rested on heavy planks overnight to stop it sinking into the sand. It carried over a thousand gallons of fuel. They had a smooth take-off from the beach. After a difficult flight, which included flying blind through fog, the Southern Cross landed at Harbour Grace in Newfoundland some thirty-one hours later. The aircraft was refuelled and following breakfast they flew the last thousand miles to New York landing at Roosevelt Field Aerodrome, Long Island to receive a hero's welcome.

Left: Michael Collins throwing in a ball to start the 1920 Leinster Hurling Final at Croke Park on 23 August 1921. The game had been postponed from 1920 following the events of Bloody Sunday, 21 November 1920, when thirteen people, including Michael Hogan, the Tipperary back, were killed by British auxiliary forces at Croke Park in retribution. In the final, Dublin beat Kilkenny.

Below: The Keating Branch of the Gaelic Football League, Parnell Square, Dublin, who were the winners of the Dublin Cup in 1909.

Opposite below: The pre-match parade for Tipperary and Wexford in the All-Ireland Hurling Final at Croke Park on 4 September 1960. Tipperary were the favourites, but Wexford went on to win the game scoring 2-15 to Tipperary's 0-11.

Above: Croke Park, *c.*1950. The Artane Boys Band plays before the start of a Gaelic football final. There are packed crowds in the Cusack Stand (called the 'double-decker stand') on the eastern side of the park. The stand was built at a cost of £52,000 and when opened, on 21 August 1938, was said to be one of the largest covered stands in the world. The upper deck had seating for 5000 people, while the lower deck was for standing only.

Belvedere College Senior Cup Team 1924, who were winners of the Leinster Schools Senior Cup.
Back Row: Paddy McAllister, Harry Tighe, Claude Carroll, Noel McAuley, Tom (Bob) O'Connell,
Eugene Crosby. Middle Row: Dan O'Connor, Michael Roche, Eddie Doyle, Kevin Keohane
(Captain), Joe Moran, Alfred Flood, David Moran. Front Row: Niall O'Rahilly, Jack Arigho.

Belvedere College Senior Cup Team 1927. Back Row, left to right: M. Walsh, P. Kevans, P. O'Leary,
L. Mangan, J. Callaghan, T. Gleeson. Middle Row: D. O'Herlihy, E. May, J. McGrath, D. Mulcahy
(Capt.), B. O'Reilly, S. Doyle, R. Sheridan. Front Row: D. Murphy, T. Hyland.

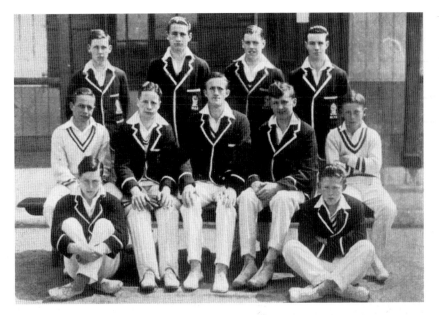

Belvedere College Senior Cricket Team, 1927. Back Row, from left to right: E. Inngram, S. Doyle, B. O'Reilly, F. Connell. Middle Row: G. Morgan, D. Mulcahy, P. O'Leary (Capt.), J. Byrne, J. Brophy. Front Row (sitting): M. Walsh, J. Boucher.

Belvedere College under 12 Cricket Team, which won all ten games played in 1957. Back Row, left to right: G. Tanham, H. Kelly, E. Fitzgerald. Middle Row: G. Lynch, B. Wilson, D. Tyndall, P. Shanley. Front Row (sitting): H. Cahill, D. Neary, P. Murphy, P. Hayes, B. Gallagher.

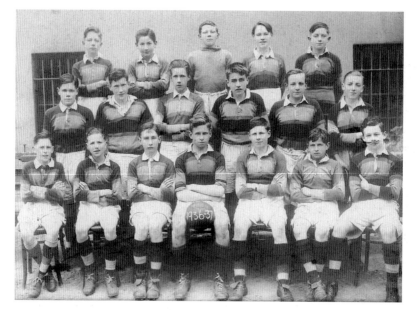

Scoil Oconaill Ath Cliath 'B' Team, Junior Football Champions C.B.S. League, 1937: Back row, left to right: S. O'Meara, S. Cusack, D. Lawler, L. Synnot, C. Byrne. Middle Row: S. Connolly, J. Conroy, D. McCarthy, H. McHale, M. Dunne, J. Tyrrell. Front Row: C. Melinn, S. Mulcahy, O. Kearns, A. Richardson (Capt.), S. Conway, S. Egan, S. Prendergast.

St. Joseph's, Fairview, under 14 Hurling Team, cup winners in 1966: Back Row, left to right: Mick Boyle, Aiden Hampson, Ciarian O'Shea, Martin Redmond, Declan Buckley, Vincent Lambe, Richie Oonan, Dermot ?. Middle Row: Gerry Coffin, Denis Cagney, John Hart, Joe Finucane, John Keevy, Eammon Daly, Tom Quinn. Front Row: Stephen Harvey, Fergie Phelan, P J Reid, Ken Fagan, Liam Twohy.

Clontarf Football Club has played at Castle Avenue since 1896. In season 1902–03 they were admitted to the Leinster League and the following year they reached the final of the Leinster Senior Cup only to lose to Lansdowne by five points to three. However, in 1936, they were winners of the Leinster Senior Challenge Cup for the first time. This is a photograph of the 1922 Cup Team. Back Row, left to right: J. A. Watts, W. Barton, D. B. Hourihan, S. P. Mercier, J. M. Quail, J. Brady, S.E. Polden (Hon. Sec.). Middle Row: J. C. Montgomery, A. Kelly, A. E. Dallas, H. S. T. Cormac (Capt.), W. L. Freeman, J. H. Hopkins, V. H. Bradley. Front Row: W. S. Corrigan, W. A. Noonan.

Clontarf Cricket Club was founded in 1876 and in 1896 they moved to the ground at Castle Avenue. They won the Junior Leinster Cup in 1898 and 1905 and were promoted to the Senior League in 1908. Since 1964, international cricket matches have been played at the ground. This is a photograph of the second Eleven in 1921. Back Row, left to right: R. Sandys, C. J. Boylan, J. N. Dollar, A. J. G. White, R. Barton. Middle Row: E. H. Verdon, W. G. Mallet, J. W. Kelly, J. Foxall, J. C. Montgomery. Front Row: J. S. Hopkins, R. A. Archer.

Loreto College, North Great Georges Street, Fourth Year Class, 1958.

Third Year Class, Mercy College, Coolock, June 1968.

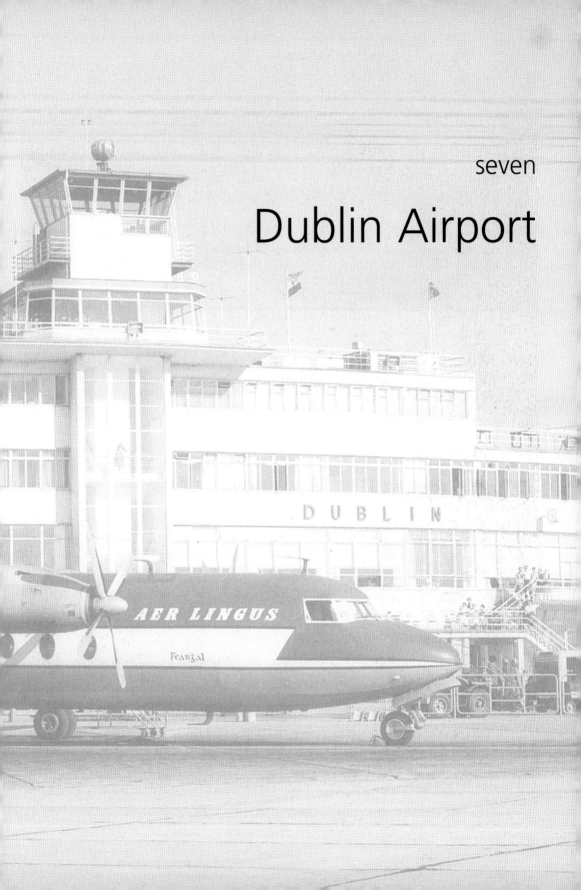

seven

Dublin Airport

Terminal Building, Collinstown Airport, Dublin, art deco style. The graceful terminal building opened in 1941. It was designed by Desmond Fitzgerald and he is thought to have modelled the terminal to resemble the bridge of a luxury liner. It had spacious balconies for spectators to view the planes. The airport was built on the site of a military aerodrome, which was in operation during the First World War. The site was ideal as Collinstown had an excellent weather record and an obstacle free approach as it was ten miles from the nearest mountains. The airport was designed in 1937 and was officially opened to air traffic on 19 January 1940. During the first year, only 10,650 passengers and less than eighteen tons of freight were handled.

Dublin Airport, Collinstown was the home base of Aer Lingus. The Aer Lingus Airline was founded in May 1936 with one five-seater De Havilland 84 Dragon named *Iolar* (Eagle), which had been bought from the Blackpool and West Coast Airline for £2,400. This plane was used by the airline until 1939. In 1936, the total Aer Lingus staff numbered twelve. The first cross channel passenger service was between Dublin and Bristol. When it opened, Dublin Airport had grass strips but hard runways soon became essential for the larger planes and three concrete runways were completed in 1950.

Dublin Airport, Collinstown, showing the approach to the terminal building and an Aer Lingus Douglas DC3 plane on the apron. The first Douglas DC3 was bought in 1940. It proved a reliable aircraft and Aer Lingus eventually increased the number to a fleet of twenty DC3s. These aircraft were used by the airline on services to Britain and Europe for around twenty-five years. In 1945, the fare from Dublin to London was £13.00 return.

An Aer Lingus Douglas DC3, St. Albert, being serviced prior to departure, from Dublin, c.1950. The plane could carry thirt-two passengers. In 1950, services operated from Dublin Airport to Shannon, the main UK airports, Paris and Amsterdam. There were also seasonal services to the Isle of Man and Jersey. However, it was not until March 1958 that radar was installed at Dublin Airport.

Above: Postcard showing the new Control Tower which was situated above the central terminal building on the eastern side of the airfield at a height some sixty-eight feet above apron level. The Aer Lingus Irish International Airlines Fokker Friendship *Feargal*, which could carry up to forty passengers, waits on the apron.

Below: Douglas (Wrong-way) Corrigan left New York in a tiny Curtis-Robins single-engine plane that cost $900 saying he was flying to California and landed at Collinstown Airport, Dublin on 18 July 1938. His flight had taken twenty-eight hours and thirteen minutes. He claimed that his 180 degree wrong turn was due to a compass malfunction and that fog had prevented him from taking a visual reading. His story was not believed, especially as he had previously applied to the Civil Aviation Authority in Los Angeles for a license to attempt a trans-Atlantic flight and been turned down. As a young man, while working at the Ryan Aircraft factory in San Diego on the plane *Spirit of St. Louis*, he had met Charles Lindberg. It is likely that he hoped to match Lindberg's feat and complete a similar flight. Although Corrigan's flight in such a small plane was successful, the aviation authorities in Ireland and America were certainly not

DOUGLAS P. CORRIGAN
and his 1929 Curtis-Robins Plane
NEW YORK to DUBLIN
July 17-18, 1938
3150 miles 28 hrs. 13 min.

impressed and his pilot's license was suspended. However, when he returned to America 'Wrong-way' Corrigan was greeted as a hero. The public admired his daring and he was welcomed back with a ticker tape parade in New York. He had a brief moment of fame and even starred in a film about his exploits *The Flying Irishman*, before retiring to California to grow oranges. He died in 1995.

eight

Portmarnock and Malahide

Above: St Doolagh's Church, Malahide, *c.*1890. This is one of Ireland's oldest churches, said to have been built by the Danes in the twelfth century. The original walls at the east end of the church are twelve feet thick, which helped to prevent the steep-pitched stone roof from collapsing. The remainder of the church including the square tower dates from the fifteenth century. St. Doolagh himself was an anchorite or hermit and in the centre there is a room measuring ten feet by seven feet in which an anchorite would live. The church also has a Bishop's room, a leper's window and a penitential cell, where a sinner would stay until he repented.

Opposite top: Motor Races at Portmarnock on the 'Velvet Strand' in September 1904. The speed trials were organised by the Irish Automobile Club. There was a good crowd, numbering around 5000, who came to watch the races. This is the start of one of the heats for the Automobile Club 200 Guinea Challenge Cup. The Irish driver, Algernon Lee Guinness is in car No. 17, on the left of the photo, and the English driver, J.W. Stocks is in car No. 37. Wooden boards are laid on the sands to make a firm platform for the start. The cars then had two miles of smooth sand on which to race.

Opposite middle: The start of the second heat in the Racing Cars Section in the Portmarnock Speed Trials in 1904. The six-cylinder Napier (No. 2), driven by Selwyn F. Edge, who had won the 1902 Gordon-Bennett Race in this car, is on the left of the photo. The British Gordon-Bennett Darracq, driven by A. Rawlinson, is on the right.

Opposite bottom: Five cars start in the 'Tourist Section' at the Portmarnock Speed Trials in 1904. The drivers are accompanied by their ladies. There is an interesting car with three wheels (reg. no. DUP 7), second from the left.

The photo shows the start in the Semi-Final for Touring Cars costing over £400. The eventual winner in this class was Algernon Lee Guinness aged twenty-one years. During his racing career, he would have many more victories, including the 1922 Tourist Trophy Race in the Isle of Man.

The circular Martello Tower at Portmarnock was one of the twenty-one towers built on the Irish coast between 1803 and 1806, costing £1800 each. They had granite walls around nine feet thick and their entrance was ten feet from the ground. There was a cannon at the top of the tower. Each tower held a small garrison and they were meant to give early warning and oppose any possible landing of Napoleon's troops. They never saw any action as the invasion never took place. This postcard, c.1950, shows the tower after its conversion into a number of apartments. Lambay Island is on the right of the picture.

Girls cycling across the bridge on Strand Road, Portmarnock c.1950. The ruins of the water-driven corn mill, which had been damaged in the storm of 1903, are on the right. The mill had been at this site for two hundred years and it was powered by the rise and the fall of the tide.

A busy scene on the Promenade at Portmarnock c.1955. Two coaches are parked on the road. This was a very popular destination for Dubliners, especially at weekends. The Great Northern Railway provided frequent bus and rail services to and from Dublin. The bandstand is in the centre and a band would play there every Sunday in July and August to entertain the crowds.

The Promenade and Beach at Portmarnock *c.*1955. There are many visitors on the beach, but there is still plenty of room for all to enjoy the sea air and the golden sands. Rides along the beach on the donkeys were a special treat for children. The Strand Café is on the far right.

Richard Talbot was a Knight who came to Ireland with Henry II in 1172. The lands and Harbour of Malahide were given to him in 1185. Malahide Castle was owned by the Talbot family from 1174 until 1976, apart from 1649 to 1660, when ownership of the castle was granted by Oliver Cromwell to Miles Corbet. The castle was once surrounded by a moat. The inner part of the building dates from the fourteenth century and there are many fine rooms including the medieval Great Hall, built around 1480, which has a Minstrel Gallery and the Oak Room which was built around 1550. Further additions to the castle include the Library and the Drawing Rooms. Fourteen members of the Talbot family are said to have had breakfast in the Great Hall before riding out to take part in the Battle of the Boyne on 1 July 1690. Sadly, none were to return, as all were killed in the battle.

Above left: Lord Talbot de Malahide, (1846-1921).

Above right: Lady Talbot de Malahide, (1851-1932).

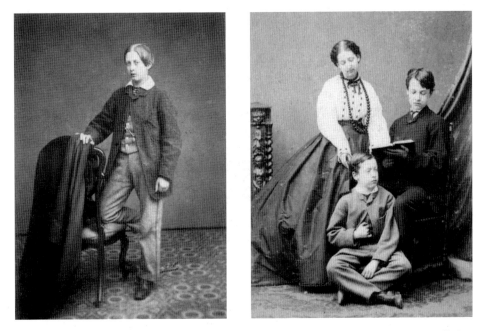

Above left: Hon. Richard Talbot who married Emily the great granddaughter of James Boswell, the biographer of Dr. Samuel Johnson.

Above right: Hon. Frances Talbot de Malahide with James and Reginald Talbot (sitting on the chair).

Hon. Milo Talbot who between 1948 and 1973 created magnificent gardens around the castle. He was the last Lord Talbot of Malahide when he died in 1973.

Left: Hon. James Talbot (1874-1948).

Opposite below: The Grand Hotel, Malahide, *c.*1910. The hotel has had several owners. It was built by James Fagan of Feltrim in 1835 and was then called the Royal Hotel. However, it was renamed the Grand Hotel, when it was purchased by H. Bethell in 1897. The next owner of note was Dr. John Colohan, who bought the hotel in 1911 for £10,000. He had a liking for pink gin and decided to paint it pink. The hotel became well known to Dubliners as the 'Pink Hotel'. Dr Colohan was also a motoring enthusiast and he is said to have brought the first petrol driven car, a Benz Comfortable, to Ireland in November 1896. He sold the hotel for £17,000 in 1918. Following this, under a number of owners, the hotel's trade diminished. Fortunately, the Grand was reconstructed and modernised in 1955 and today is a thriving hotel with an international reputation.

Above: The Diamond, Malahide, *c.*1912. In the early nineteenth century, there was a water fountain in the centre of the Diamond, but this was removed to allow stagecoaches to easily reach the Grand Hotel when it opened in 1835. The postcard shows the steeple of St. Sylvester's Church on the right and jaunting cars on the road. Two constables from the Royal Irish Constabulary (RIC) stand on the pavement on the left. The policeman furthest away is standing outside the RIC Barracks. Around 1912, Malahide had a population of 1,300 and the RIC Barracks was manned by Sergeant. J. Sweeney and four constables.

St James' Terrace, Malahide, *c.*1903. This regency styled terrace was built by James Fagan around 1835, as seaside homes for wealthy Dubliners. The last house, at the sea end, was traditionally rented by the Officer-in-Charge of the Coast Guard Station.

Malahide Coast Road and Strand, *c.*1915. On the left stands the converted Martello Tower with its conical roof with superb views over the beach and estuary. The Martello Tower conversion was designed by the architect F.G. Hicks in 1910 for his own home and it became known as 'Hick's Tower'.

The Shipyard, Malahide, c.1950. Since the early 1900s Malahide always had a small boatyard. This built some fine wooden yachts, but the boatyard mainly concentrated on the repair and maintenance of local yachts and fishing boats. In the 1950s, when the yard came under new ownership, it was decided to focus on building new Malahide Trawler Yachts. This venture was very successful. Sales gradually increased so that, by the late 1960s and early 1970s, there were boom times for the yard, which trebled in size. However, in the later 1970s, oil crises, inflation and cheaper competitors in the Far East reversed the trend and the shipyard declined, finally closing in 1983. A large apartment complex now stands on the site, overlooking a 300 berth marina.

The boat landing stage and Island Golf Links, Malahide, c.1950. The Island Golf Club was founded on land leased from the Cobbe Estate in 1890. It had ten founder members and for many years golfers took a 500 yard boat trip from this slip way to the links golf course on the island. The boatman would know to collect the golfers when a large red and white disc was displayed on the island, which could be seen from the shore. However, the ferry service was discontinued in 1973 and today golfers make the journey to the peninsula by car.

Malahide Cricket Club, 1945. Winners of the Senior Cup Division 2.

Malahide Cricket Club, 1948. Winners of the Senior (Division 2) League and Cup.

nine

Swords, Donabate, Lusk and Rush

The Castle, Swords, *c*.1905. The castle, located at the north end of Swords Main Street, was built in 1183 by John Comyn, the first Norman Archbishop of Dublin, for use as his Summer Palace. It has five sides, which enclose a large courtyard, with a tower on the north side and a strong gateway on the south side. The Archbishop held a weekly court at the castle. Punishments were severe and over the years many criminals were hanged at Gallows Hill. The castle was vulnerable in the military sense and sustained a lot of damage when it was attacked by Edward Bruce and his Scottish army in 1316. This probably explains why the Dublin Archbishop of the time left Swords to go to a new palace at Tallaght in 1324. Swords was a market town and regular sales of crops and livestock took place there. Every year on the feast of St. Columcille a fair was held in Swords which lasted for eight days. Queen Elizabeth I gave the town municipal rights in 1578.

The Main Street, Swords, *c*.1910. Swords is the most ancient town in County Dublin and has its origin in an extensive Abbey founded by St Columcille around 560. The first Abbott was St. Fionan Lobar and under his leadership Swords became a treatment centre for leprosy. The monastery was the overnight resting place for the bodies of Brian Boru and his son Murtagh after the Battle of Clontarf before they were taken on to Armagh for burial. In 1910, the town consisted of one wide street about a mile in length. The Castle can be seen on the left at the far end of the street. The grocery shop on the left is owned by John Coleman.

Lower Street (North Street), Swords, *c*.1910. A young boy stands by the hand-operated village water pump, which is on the right. This is the water pump which is mentioned in chapter 17 of *Ulysses*, when James Joyce surmises 'had Bloom and Stephen been baptised under a pump in the village of Swords?'.

St Patrick's Church, Donabate, *c*.1920. The church, which opened in 1903, was built of red brick on a site donated by John Smyth the owner of the Bridge Public House. The altar has stone carvings which tell the story of St Patrick. There are two fine stained glass windows in the church. There is a rose window, which shows angels playing different musical instruments and also another window, *Suffer little children* designed by the Dublin stained glass artist Harry Clarke (1889-1931), which was presented by the Men's Sodality in 1925.

Above: Donabate Strand, *c.*1955. The Martello Tower is on the left. This was built in 1830 and was the sixth in the series of towers built on the coast for defence against possible French attack. Lambay Island is in the distance on the right of the picture. There are a few parked cars as families enjoy playing on this fine sandy beach.

Lusk Village, *c*.1950. A later view of the village shows that the cottage in front of the church no longer has a thatched roof and the left half of the cottage has been converted to the village shop. The village water pump is to the left of the telegraph pole outside the shop. Today the Lusk Heritage Centre is beside the tower.

Above: Lower Main Street, Rush *c*.1905. There is a long main street extending from the Harbour. Children play in the street, which has many thatched cottages.

Opposite below: Lusk, county Dublin, *c*.1900. A view of the village, painted by the artist 'Jotter', showing an idyllic scene with picturesque thatched cottages. The population at that time was around 220. Lusk is one of the oldest ecclesiastical settlements in Ireland dating from the fifth century when a monastery was founded by St. MacCulin. Records show a fairly continuous line of Abbots and Bishops in occupation there until the Norman invasion. The only remaining part of this Celtic Abbey is the Round Tower (without its conical cap), which is ninety-five feet high and has walls which are four feet thick. There are remains of Norman battlements, a medieval belfry and a church built in 1859, on the site of Lusk Abbey. There is a very elaborate memorial to Sir Christopher Barnewall of Turvey and his wife in the church.

Upper Main Street, Rush, *c.*1912. There are fewer thatched cottages. At that time the population of Rush was around 1,300 people. There were 320 houses and the only public buildings were the Roman Catholic Church and the Martello Tower on the beach. Many of the indigenous Rush families are descended from Norsemen who settled there in the ninth and tenth centuries.

The Square, Rush, *c.*1910. Children play in the street outside the white thatched cottages. The village water pump is in front of the cottage on the right. The distinctive cast-iron pump was hand-operated and had decorated panels.

Rush Village, *c.*1910. A peaceful scene with schoolchildren playing by the telegraph pole. The village pump is just seen on the far right of the photograph. The writer of the card says she is 'having good fun and a lovely time camping with the guides'.

Coastguard Station, Rush *c.*1912. This is the building on the right of the picture, which stood by the harbour. At that time, the officer in command was H. Norton. The Coastguard Station together with those at Skerries, Loughshinny and Lusk was burnt down in the Troubles in 1921.

Many of the thatched cottages in north Dublin were allowed to fall into disrepair. Here schoolchildren play in the road outside a cottage, which is in much need of attention.

The Harbour, Rush, c.1910. The pier was built by the Duke of Ormonde to help protect the harbour, which was not easy to access, particularly in north-east winds. In the mid-eighteenth century there were around forty vessels based in Rush harbour. Most were occupied in fishing and Rush was well known for the quality of its salted cod. However, as was found in many of the north Dublin coastal harbours, some vessels would be involved in smuggling, particularly tea, brandy and tobacco. Famous Rush smugglers in the late eighteenth century were Captain Luke Ryan and Jack 'The Bachelor' Connor.

ten

Skerries and
Balbriggan

Holmpatrick Church of Ireland and Pool Skerries, *c*.1905. A horse-drawn delivery cart from William Ennis Mills Bakery stands in the water. The two delivery men are Tom Halligan and T. Moles. At that time there were two bakeries in Skerries. They were the Mill Bakery and Landy's Lane Bakery.

Strand Street, Skerries, *c*.1910. This was the main shopping street and Thom's Directory for 1912 has a number of traders living in the street including two butchers, two farriers, three drapers, four grocers and spirit merchants, Mrs Grime's tea rooms, Shelley and Shea newsagents and William Ennis, miller and baker. The monument is at the far end of the street and there are thatched cottages on the left.

Strand Street, Skerries, Co. Dublin.

View of Strand Street showing the Monument and the Grand Hotel, *c.*1945. The original hotel premises were leased from Ion Hamilton by William Morris in 1873 and later extended on several occasions. There was a succession of owners who carried on the grocery and provisions trade as well as the hotel business. However, in June 1948 the De La Salle Brothers bought the Grand Hotel for £14,000. It was then converted into a house for the Brothers and the De La Salle Secondary School for boys. There was also a small preparatory school. Today the De La Salle School and the Convent School run by the Holy Faith Sisters have closed and the pupils from both schools attend St Patrick's Senior National School.

Church Street, Skerries, *c.*1912. The Bell Tower and west end of St Patrick's Catholic Church is seen in the centre. The church was built in 1832 with the entrance in Church Street, which was the main street at the time. The belfry, designed by Mr. J. O'Callaghan and built of local Milverton limestone, was added in 1834. Thom's Directory shows only one doctor in Skerries in 1912, who was Dr B. P. Healy, who lived at 'Seapark', in Church Street.

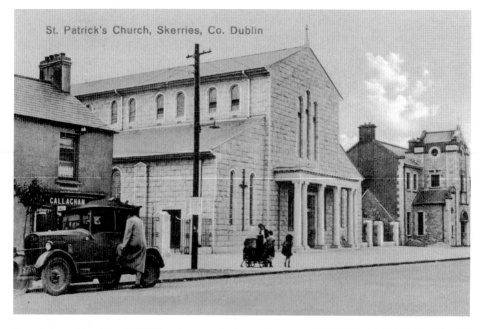

St. Patrick's Church, Skerries, Co. Dublin

Strand Street, Skerries, *c*.1940. The photograph shows the east end of St. Patrick's Catholic Church, which was built on the same site with only the belfry retained from the previous church. The new church took four years to build and was consecrated in 1939. On the right of the church is the Carnegie Public Library. This was designed by Anthony and William Scott and built in 1910, using limestone from Milverton Quarry. It is one of the many libraries built in Ireland with grants from Andrew Carnegie. He was Scottish, but emigrated to America with his parents in 1848, where he made his fortune. He returned to Scotland in 1901 and used his wealth to help build and equip libraries in these Isles. He died in 1919 at the age of eighty-four.

Cross St. & Balbriggan St. Skerries

Cross Street and Balbriggan Street, Skerries, *c*.1920. The photographer has caught everybody's attention. At that time, Skerries had many attractive thatched cottages and some can be seen at the street junction.

Windmill Hill, Skerries, c.1905. The windmill has just three remaining sails. The man holding the spare blade and watching as the field of hay is cut is Jack Attley, who worked at the mill. There were windmills at Skerries dating back to the early sixteenth century. From 1821 to 1839, there were two working windmills. There was a watermill with water coming from a large mill pond and a five-sail windmill. There was also a bakery on the site from the mid-nineteenth century. However, stone ground milling declined and by the early twentieth century the watermill was the only working mill and by 1963 it had also ceased operation. Fortunately, in 1989, Skerries Mills were purchased by Dublin County Council and have through various agencies been extensively refurbished, forming an industrial and heritage centre. Today they are a great tourist attraction.

The Mill Cottage and the Mill, Skerries on a postcard dated August 1912. There are three sails on the windmill.

A peaceful scene in the Harbour, Skerries, *c*.1910. A young boy sits on the quay and a solitary fisherman stands on his boat. The building in the centre of the picture next to the white house is the lifeboat house, which was built in 1903. The harbour is one of the best on this part of the coast as it is very sheltered from south-west gales.

Above: The Harbour and Guest House, Skerries, *c*.1940. Spectators line the Harbour walls as some young swimmers prepare for the start of a race. Skerries Swimming Club was founded in 1924 and the club organised these races each Summer.

Opposite below: A group of children (the 'Waterwags') on Skerries beach, shown on a card posted to Kilkee on 28 August 1901.

Above: During the 1920s, there was an annual regatta and swimming gala held at Skerries. Yachts came to compete in the regatta from Howth, Clontarf and Dun Laoghaire. Swimmers would come from Skerries and all over County Dublin. The Regatta Committee would block off Harbour Road and would charge sixpence to view the races. Following a disagreement between the Regatta Committee and the Skerries Swimming Club in the 1930s the groups went their separate ways. However, Skerries continued to hold a swimming gala and this photo shows a swimming race in the Harbour at Skerries, *c.*1945.

The Sea Water Baths on the South Strand, *c*.1905, as rebuilt after the fire in 1902. The baths and recreation hall was originally built by William Flanagan. The baths were used to teach swimming to children from Skerries and did not close until 1922. Later this building was to become The Pavilion Cinema and the hall were used for entertaining the holiday crowds with concerts, plays and travelling shows. Entertainers included the famous tenor Count John McCormack, Jimmy O'Dea, Percy French and Cyril Cusack. When the ballroom was extended in 1949, many famous show bands played there including the local *Graduates Showband*.

Above: Families on the Sands at Skerries in 1905. Unfortunately, the weather has not been kind and all are well wrapped up. However, there are bathing huts further up the beach and these would be used by visitors during the hot summer days, when the sun shone and the sea was warm.

Opposite below: The Captain's Bathing Place, Skerries, *c*.1910. There was good deep water here, which made it a very popular place for experienced swimmers. The rocks were also perfect for relaxing and sunbathing. The deep pool between the Captain's and the Springboards was called the Mackerel Pit.

GENTOURS BOYS CAMP, SKERRIES.

R 2902

Above: Gentours Boys Camp, Skerries. In the Summer months, young people would come here for holidays. It was also a favourite venue for the 'Annual Camp' for many Dublin scout groups.

The Captains Bathing Place Skerries

JV 66232

Spring Board, Skerries. Co. Dublin.

Springboards, Skerries, c.1910. This was a favourite swimming spot on Red Island, as it had wooden diving boards. The Skerries Visitors' Association built the Springboards bathing place and the Captain's bathing place. Women were only allowed to use the bathing places for two hours each day. It was common to see girls sitting patiently on the rocks watching the boys, but also waiting for their turn. It was not until the late 1940s that men and women were allowed to bathe or swim at the Springboards at the same time. Today there are no wooden diving boards as the council deemed them to be too dangerous in these litigious times.

THE HARBOUR, SKERR   20080

Fishing vessels moored in the Harbour, Skerries, c.1910. A young girl poses for the photographer. Towards the end of the eighteenth century Skerries was one of the main fishing ports in Ireland. However, the number of fishing boats using the harbour gradually declined and by 1859 there were just twelve boats based in the harbour. Schooners also used the harbour to load freight and the main export from Skerries was limestone from Milverton Quarry.

Terry O'Toole (fourth from the left in the front row) and a group of his friends from Carlow at the Red Island Holiday Camp in Summer 1956. Next to Terry sitting in the chair is Sean Byrne and behind him, at the end of the second row, is Pat Hart. The camp buildings looked fairly basic, but all the rooms had sea views and central heating. Moreover, the guests enjoyed good food and great fun, with much laughter, music and dancing. Many visitors would return year after year. The favourite venue for dancers was the old Tower Ballroom by the Martello Tower, where there was live music from bands each night. There were also concerts at the camp and Terry remembers hearing a great concert during the week he was there given by Sir John Barbarolli and the Halle Orchestra.

The Lounge and Soda Fountain at Red Island, Skerries in July 1952. The camp had a dance hall, theatre, miniature golf course. The owner, Eamonn Quinn, also built the chair-lift in Bray in 1950. Every Tuesday, visitors to the Red Island holiday Camp were given the opportunity to spend a day out to Bray, which would include a ride on the chair-lift to the Eagle's Nest Café for lunch.

The Hosiery Mills, Balbriggan, taken from the Viaduct *c*.1925. Balbriggan was known worldwide for quality hosiery. The upper and lower large cotton mills and a fine pier and harbour were built in the second half of the eighteenth century by the Hamilton family with the help of grants from the Irish Parliament. This brought great prosperity to Balbriggan, which was transformed from a fishing village to a thriving industrial town.

A row of young girls making fine texture hosiery in the Smyth and Company factory at Balbriggan *c*.1895. Natural light and gas lighting was used in the factory. The quality underwear they produced was highly regarded and silk stockings were made on a special loom in the factory for Queen Victoria throughout her reign. Stockings and tights (long-johns) were widely known as 'Balbriggans'.

The Banks, Balbriggan on a postcard dated 15 October 1906. On the upper right of the photograph are the walls of the Martello Tower. The St. Patrick's Band is seen playing on the left. This was a very popular band, which performed regularly between 1906 and 1916 on Sundays on the Banks at Balbriggan.

The Banks, Balbriggan on a postcard dated 15 November 1911. The new bandstand is seen near the shore on the right. Behind the bandstand is the Martello Tower and to the left is the Coastguard Station, which has a conical roof.

Other titles published by Nonsuch

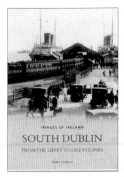

Images of Ireland: South Dublin
DEREK STANLEY

From the Liffey riverside to the picturesque coastal scenery, this book is a fascinating collection of old photographs and postcards that chart the past century of South Dublin's history.

1-84588-566-X

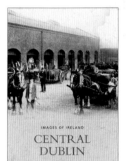

Images of Ireland: Central Dublin
DEREK STANLEY

Dublin is a vibrant and modern European capital city, with a long distinguished history dating back to the time of the Vikings. This book displays the immense character of the city centre through a striking collection of photographs and postcards.

1-84588-567-8

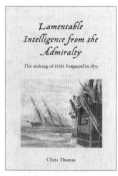

Lamentable Intelligence from the Admirality
CHRIS THOMAS

HMS Vanguard sank in thick fog in Dublin Bay in September 1875. The unjust verdict handed down by the Court Martial marked this incident as significant in naval history. This book revisits the sinking, exploring the joys and trials of seagoing life in the Victorian era.

1-84588-544-9

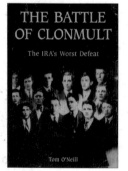

The Battle of Clonmult
TOM O'NEILL

The 1921 Battle of Clonmult is known as the IRA's worst defeat. This book provides an insight into the days preceding the battle and the progress of the battle itself and is an invaluable guide to the history of the IRA in Cork.

1-84588-554-6

If you are interested in purchasing other books published by Nonsuch, or in case you have difficulty finding any Nonsuch books in your local bookshop, you can also place orders directly through our website

www.nonsuch-publishing.com